T0381221

THE SILENT TEACHERS

PRYAMVADA BANN

Balboa Press books may be ordered through booksellers or by contacting:

Balboa Press
A Division of Hay House
1663 Liberty Drive
Bloomington, IN 47403
www.balboapress.com
1 (877) 407-4847

ISBN: 978-1-5043-4329-9 (sc)
ISBN: 978-1-5043-4330-5 (e)

Library of Congress Control Number: 2015918189

Print information available on the last page.

Balboa Press rev. date: 10/14/2017

BALBOA
PRESS
A DIVISION OF HAY HOUSE

Paintings by Pryam Bann

The Pearl Necklace Painting by Samantha Soucy

DEDICATION

To Mama and Pappy
They taught me the meaning of the word love

To my three sisters
Their presence taught me many of Life's Lessons

To my three daughters
Rana Nanda Samantha
For the privilege of giving me the precious gift of motherhood

To my Ex-husband
I thank him for giving me the gift of family

To my grandchildren
Allowing me to have a sense of evolution and immortality

To Dr. R. Routhier
Whose words gave me the courage to trust,
That all will be well…

Kyra, I thank you so much for your patience
And your gifted knowledge in aiding to put
This project together…

To all the people who supported me financially
I shall always be grateful and I thank you with
My love…

A warm and embracing thank you to my cousin Virraj Bann
for the Waterfall experience

CONTENTS

PREFACE

I call this book The Silent Teachers, because I have discovered that

If I pay attention to nature and things, they have unique and subtle

Ways of teaching valuable lessons in life.

These lessons have affected me in life changing ways. I wish to share

These stories with you in hopes that you too will discover your own

Silent Teachers…

Eg: - observing Bees buzzing about their business told me that

Life must go on after tragedy strikes…

While taking a walk in the woods, coming across a piece of discarded snake

skin told me that we must shed our pain in order to see our purpose clearly.

-My grandfather's kaleidoscope has taught me to treasure the uniqueness

In people I encounter

I invite you to connect the higher self thru nature and things

then pay attention to how you feel…

Love and Light
Pryam

RHYTHM OF THE RAIN

Rain falls on the branches

of a rose shrub

Drops…tap tap tapping

on the canopy, creating the sound

Causing the leaves

to dance to the rhythm of a soft and gentle shower

Allowing me to pause for a moment

And become one with nature…

2

MAMA

When death closed the door to my heart

I listened to the silent interval of change…

Mind, Body and Spirit

seemed disconnected

The womb which gave birth to me

was no longer warm with life

Yet I did not want to let her go

As the days went by…

I remembered

Nothing remains the same

It was time to make

My own footprints

On the sands of Mother Earth

I also remembered

Love is the energy

which heals the heart

In order to reconnect

The Mind, Body and Spirit

Looking around

I sought out love

-The unexpected twittering of a bird,

My children's laughter at play

Gave tugs to my heart

-Walking along the garden and stopping to smell a rose

gave me the promise of hope

-Observing the bees on my flowering crab apple tree

buzzing about their business

Told me

Life must go on…

Little by little

My heart began to open

and the pain of losing my Dear Mama

Subsided…

Death is the realization

Of the sacredness of life

We as humans---possess a driving ambition

To become something better than ourselves

Surviving the death of my Earthly Mother

Has led me to the belief

Life is most fragile and precious

Look forward to change

For change is the act of

Leaping into the experience of life

And living life

And loving life

Is the energy and heartbeat

That sustains our World and Beyond…

WHAT IF

As we unfold this enigma

Called Life

A thought comes to mind

What if what we think of as being real

Is actually a Dream

A dream whose purpose is

To teach us

The meaning of being human and

To reconnect to the truth of who we really are

What if we are innately

Spiritual in Nature

But in order to survive on this planet

We have to learn to adapt

To this human form of

Mind and body

This would explain

Why we are so inept at being human

We pride ourselves in being

An intelligent species

Yet ignoring that part of us

Which reminds us of who we instinctively are

We call this enigma

-The Subconscious

-Intuition

-Love

-Creativity

What if this dream

Leads us to an existence

Of combining

Both, the physical and Spiritual dimensions

Living in a realm of possibilities…

This thought makes me believe

That there is more to the human condition

Than what we See, Hear, Touch, Taste and Smell

And what if the Universe (God)

Gives us clues to our instinctive existence

-Appreciating the beauty in everything we see

-To become inspired by the sound

Of our favourite piece of music

-To softly touch the cheek, of a new born babe

-To savor the taste of a sumptuous meal

-And inhaling

The intoxicating aroma of a beloved flower...

We never feel alone

Giving attention to these moments

I believe

That love and creativity

Is the energy which nudges us

To connect the human self to our Spiritual Nature

Unto the path

Of our Evolutionary Awakening...

INTENTIONS

A thought passes through the mind

No attention is given

It was as if gently being kissed on the cheek by the wind

The thought passes through the mind once again

Becoming an acquaintance

Bringing a smile to one's face

The thought continues to envelope the mind

Until it feels like you are greeting an old friend

Then it starts dancing in your head

Until it becomes an idea

Weighing the pros and cons…

Until one or the other feels right

and so escalates into an intention

This intention awakens into

Something that is no longer dormant

But…alive

Transforming: Like a cocoon into a butterfly

To land where it may…

LIVING IN THE NOW

Looking at the bright morning sky

I am distracted by the arrival of a beautiful bird

perching on the tip of a tree

outside my window

My knees become weak with fear

as he sways back and forth

on that tiny branch

He begins to twist from East to West

Singing his song of praise

Welcoming the New Day with pure joy

I marvel at his surefootedness

No regrets of days gone by

No worries of what tomorrow may bring

No fear of stumbling or falling

Providing me with a lesson on…

Living in the Now

14

THE BEAUTIFUL BIRD

He exuded such clarity and confidence from being in the moment

My desire is to be like him

Unafraid and living life to the fullest

Whenever my mind regresses to the past

Or jumps ahead into the future

And I am not living in the now

I recall that little beautiful bird

Take a deep breath

Then bring myself in the present moment

With no fear of the past or of the future…

A GLIMMER OF HOPE

The mind floods with confusion

The body feels trapped

Reverberating uncertainty

Losing my sense of balance

Wishing that the drowning pain of hopelessness

could stop

The body reaches a point of no return

Tears wash the emotions

Until the mind can grasp

at a moment of stillness

Exercising the power of choice

Do I run?

Do I weather the storm

Opting for hope gives me the strength to face adversity

Hope ebbs and flows

Like the waters along the seashore

Sometimes lapping at the sand

Other times coming in like a tempest

Why do I cling to hope

Is it because I am waiting for the fog to clear

In order to see the truth?

Is it because of the fear of change

Or delving into the unseen future?

Hope gives me the opportunity to be creative

And to deal with my fears and doubts

It gives time and space to gather my thoughts

And take an active part in personal growth

I don't know where hope will take me

For it is as elusive as:

Trying to hold on to a beautiful sunset

Before the dark

Whether the outcome works for or against my wishes

Only time will tell

For it is during the stormy period

my sense of balance is tested and choices are made

The beauty here is:

Choosing to ride out the storm

While allowing love to guide me on this journey…

I have a chance to discover more about

My strengths and weaknesses

I attain a little wisdom along the way

So I would conclude:

Just a glimmer of hope

Is worth the lessons we choose to learn…

A PIECE OF CANVAS

With brush in hand

The mind focuses on

Hues, shapes, colours and textures

Of a breath-taking sunset

Emotions overflow in awe

Feelings of unworthiness seep in

Yet being thankful to the Universe for the gift of sight

to behold such beauty

This is the power of true love

It is not meant to be possessed

It is not meant to get attached to

It is meant to be shared

Amongst all creatures on this planet

Now! How do I bring this to life

On a piece of canvas

SHEDDING THE PAST

When I was three

I did not remember

Suckling at my mother's breasts as a babe

When I was five

I did not recall

Crawling on the floor

Before I could walk

At the age of thirteen

I searched my mind and came up with a blank:

How and when did I comprehend

How to read and write

As I grew

The memory of those milestones

Were no longer important

And that part of me died

If this is death,

Then there is nothing to fear but fear itself…

While taking a walk in the forest one day

I came upon

The discarded skin of a snake

At every stage of its maturity

The snake shakes off the past as it ages…

The difference between the snake and us is:

The snake does not bring along the weight of his past

On the other hand

Humans often carry the weight

Of pain and suffering into adulthood…

Obscuring the way we see our world and each other

In order to live our lives in peace and harmony

We must shed the layers of pain and suffering

It is only then can we discover

What it truly means to be human

We shed the memory of suckling

We shed the memory of what it felt like

From crawling to walking

We shed the memory of how and when we learned to read and write

And when we shed the memory

Of pain and suffering of our past

Only then can we have

A clear vision

To fulfilling our purpose

With grace and gratitude...

WITHIN THE FOG

You cry tears of disappointment

Instead of dusting yourself off and trying again

You re-live the sob stories of a painful past

Instead of taking the opportunity to learn

Life's valuable lessons

Because you feel that

Life has been unfair

You live life with an air

Of entitlement and arrogance

You stoop to addiction

To numb the shame of lies and deceptions

When all you have to do is:

Reach inward

Step into the light and touch love…

THE PEARL NECKLACE

A gift is placed

On the palms of my open hands

I gaze upon its beauty

Cooing at the velvety touch

As I run my fingers along each pearl

Clasping the necklace around my neck

Thoughts linger on the small creatures

Whose creations are so exquisite and perfect

On closer examination and to my surprise

The pearls are not perfect

To think that a grain of sand (an irritant)

In an oyster's shell

Could create such magnificence

Is a miracle in itself

When strung together

These imperfections are of no significance

Only beauty is perceived

When looking at a person's lifespan

Imagine each pearl

Representing a year of our existence

On an invisible string of time

Gather all the years into a circle of life

The irritations and imperfections

Only enhances

What it means to be human

The flaws are what make us unique and interesting

When we place ourselves in the center of

Light and Love

Our compassionate nature shines through

Allowing us to see and be

The true magnificence in ourselves

And each other…

29

THE SILENT TEACHER

The air is filled with a scent of Spring

The time of dormancy has melted away

Ambling towards a tree

My eyes gladden at the sight of green on the branches

of an apple tree

My attention zooms in

On the twists and turns

Of its interesting gnarly trunk

A shroud of emotions beckon the senses

If you could speak

I whisper

What tales you could tell

I dream of the gift to come…

Of biting into a crisp, sweet succulent apple

To awaken the reaction of sated euphoria

But I must wait...

You give without asking for anything in return

You allow anyone to pick and enjoy your fruits

Without judgement

You provide life's sustaining oxygen

And I ask myself

What can I do to show my gratitude

You may not be able to speak

But you have taught me

The secret of

Living in harmony

Give: When it is in my power to do so

Without expectations

Stop: myself from judging others

And with patience

Truth will be realized

With a knowing smile on my face

You speak volumes in your silence...

You are a constant reminder of our connectedness

With the

Magical and Mysterious Universe…

I humbly thank you for this

Gentle and profound

Push…

A WINDOW OF LIGHT

As a child

When no one was looking

I would sneak into my Grandfather's room

Remove his kaleidoscope which was placed upon a shelf

Us children weren't allowed to play with it

because it was very fragile and could break

My Grandfather bought us plastic ones

But I enjoyed his better…

The colours were more vibrant

With no one around

I would place it up against my eye

Point it towards the light and

Enter a whole different world

The patterns of colour and light

Would delight every part of my Being…

33

I would turn the wheel

Ever so slightly while mourning the shift

Of pattern that was about to die

I would try to keep the memory of such beauty

alive in my heart

As I looked forward to seeing the new pattern

Of colors and light

I would sometimes get caught by him

And he would say

You should not be playing with that

But there was always

A hidden smile on his face

As if he knew exactly how I felt

When he too would look through that window

To discover

New patterns, colours and light

To tickle the soul…

Today I have my own kaleidoscope

Given to me by my children

They must have felt the glee on my face

Each time I told this story

They bought me a kaleidoscope exactly like my Grandfather's

It too sits on a shelf

I allow my grandchildren to gently play with it

They too enter a world of possibilities,

Delighting in colours, shapes and the joy of fleeting light…

So too we must look upon each other

With joy in our hearts

Because we do not know

when this pattern of Life would cease to exist…

CHAOS TO CALM

The further I walk into the woods

The less noise I want to make

The sound of my footsteps upon the rustling leaves

Becoming too loud…

Slowing my pace

I begin to pay attention to the sharp crags

On the bark of an aged tree

Tiny creatures busy about their business

Pay no heed to my curious eyes

As I walk along

My attention is focused on the smooth trunk

Of another tree, and so I stop

Placing my hands around its trunk

I feel an urge to put my cheek upon its bark

And so I do…

It is cool and comforting

A feeling of renewed strength

Washes over me

I am ready to face another day

With sunshine in my heart and gratitude

For my existence…

LUNA

I received my kitten

On the evening of a blue moon

Luna seemed an apt name

Her character of spurts of erratic energy

Prompted me to call her Loonie

Her soothing purring and warm soft fur

Brings a sense of peace

She then becomes Luna Belle…

My trusted friend

BE CAREFUL WHAT YOU WISH FOR

When you witness a beautiful sunset

Recall the cherished moments

When darkness falls

Be still

It is in this place of stillness

The mind and heart explore possibilities

We make conscious and most times unconscious choices

Remember:

The light will come in

Sometimes as a gentle flicker of a burning candle

At times

Like a massive explosion of distruction

And other times

Sharp and precise as a laser beam

And only you have the power to choose

In this ever changing game…called…life

40

IN THE FIELD OF POSSIBILITIES

Off in the distance

I hear the sound of a beating drum

Its rhythm captures the emotions as I get closer

Vibrations beckon me to dance

My heart and rhythm

Becoming one

Neither here nor there

Nothing and everything matters

I see your truth

I see my truth

They are but one

It is love we seek

And love we wish to give and receive…

The drumming stops

Returning me to my five sensory self

To live and breathe in a five sensory world

My purpose is clear

I am to be a student

I am to be a teacher

And when I need guidance

All I have to do is

Close my eyes

Hear the beating of a drum

And dance to the sound of its rhythm…

LIVING IN A BLACK AND WHITE WORLD

I see the pain and confusion in your eyes

Just like the bird who urges her young

With squawks of encouragement to fly

So too I must squawk

Words of encouragement in order for you to

discover a greater self…

You see the world in black and white

Take a look around and see it isn't so

The world is made up of a myriad of colours

And so too is the human journey

When you realize this

The rewards far outweigh the idea of

Living in a black and white world

I cannot exist in a world limited to the five senses…

It constricts my compassion and creativity

I need the physical as well as the spiritual

It saddens me to see you in such pain and confusion

I would like to invite you into my world

Where fear is transformed into love

Judgement into acceptance

I wish you to use your experiences

Good and Bad of the past

To be one of lessons learned and taught

I have one request of you

Do not hate me

For it is a useless emotion

You will only be hurting yourself...

So please be gentle

When thoughts of me enter your heart

Know that I love you

And wish you could love me too...

FACED WITH CHANGE

There is always an element of fear

When faced with change

The chameleon seems to wrap itself around

Obstacles it encounters in his environment

Changing its colour with such ease

Knowing that everything is unfolding as it should

When I take a look at pivotal moments in my life

It is because of change

I am who I am in this moment in time

I look back at my own history

And see a life well spent

My mind is at peace

I feel the need to embrace change

Knowing that everything is unfolding as it should…

THE VOICE OF EXPERIENCE

With hands over ears muffling sound

I hear the waves of the ocean

Scrubbing grains of sand, as they tumble towards the shore

With eyes closed

I can see

Fat, white, fluffy snow flakes falling upon my face

then melting into icy water to tickle my fancy

The sight of a Bakery brings me the aroma of

Biting into a slice of warm bread with butter

To savor each bite as a gift from the Gods…

Standing under a Willow Tree

I touch the mysterious power of your age old wisdom

and my body shivers with joy

Walking along the road on a hot summer's day

I smell the heat rising into nostrils

Creating a mirage in the distance

I can see water undulating on the asphalt

To quench my thirst

I hear the sound of a brook as it rushes by

Tasting cool clear liquid as it coats my parched throat

The scent of grass and moisture tells me

Life is thriving here

Hearing the ocean thru muffling sound…

Seeing the snowflakes falling upon my face with closed eyes

Smelling the aroma of baked bread by the sight of a Bakery

Touching the powers of the Willow with my emotions

And tasting water that isn't there…

The voice of experience speaks

Loud and clear

GROWING OLD

Here I am

In the womb of the one

I will call mother

Awaiting my entry into this world

I am in the cocoon

Anxious to start this adventure called life

The summers of my life brought many experiences in

Learning and teaching of how to function

On this spinning Orb we call Earth

Hiking in the woods on a crisp October day

I marvel at the Maple Trees

The sun

Magnifying vibrant reds, oranges and yellows

I stop

With arms wide open to the sky

Slowly spinning around

I see death, gently falling

And I think to myself

"This is awesome"

Hearing the crunching beneath my feet

I am aiding in creating fertile soil

So even in death

There is a greater purpose

Winter:

Time to sleep it seems

But this is where the magic takes hold

Metamorphosis

Like the pine trees

Discarding their needles when not required

So too I must discard memories that no longer

serve me

I must turn experiences of pain and suffering

As loam for the mind

To build a meaningful existence

Humans mirror the reflections of nature

We return to our true selves

Bringing rich knowledge and substance to our being

If growing old means experiencing death

Then I feel honoured

I give this body to Mother Earth in

Loving gratitude

So that I may serve a greater purpose

WHEN THE SOUL CRIES OUT
(INTO THE RAINFOREST)

It had been a year since major surgery

Dealing with the flow of blood going thru the heart

To nourish this human self.

Having always been drawn to water,

I looked forward with eager delight in visiting a waterfall

Described to me by my cousin

It started off as a sunny, hot and humid morning

Keeping in mind my great sense of fear of frogs and repulsion

To mud, My cousin, machete in hand, rope around his torso,

First aid kit in his backpack

A short lesson on if we encountered the only deadly snake in this region…

Into the forest we trudged

Sometimes slipping and sliding on loose gravel

Other times climbing steep hills

As sporadic raindrops washed our bodies

At times we had to stop because

My cousin had to cut a path with his machete

At one point he stopped, unshouldered his rope

Explaining that after the rainy season

The trails can change…tying one end to a tree

I said to myself

"No this is not happening"

But the drive to continue was too strong

Climbing down the rope

While trying not to get dirty from the mud in front of my face

Balancing the weight of my body with the tips of my running shoes

I forgot about getting dirty

And thought to myself

"This is fun"

There were times when I felt

I just couldn't go on and thoughts of turning back entered my mind

Others in the group

Some half my age were voicing their discomfort

And wanted to turn back

So I could have easily given up…

A Big, Blue, Beautiful Butterfly fluttering around our little group

Grabbed my attention

The sight of him replenished my energy

And gave courage to this body to carry on while

Asking myself

"Why am I doing this?"

Every time I would think of turning back

This Butterfly would appear

From the thick, lush, green forest and my heart would be gladdened

With renewed energy

While simultaneously

Hearing an echo of my Doctor's voice saying:

"If you want to get better, you must push yourself every day."

And so I carried on…

After what seemed like a long time of hiking in silence

With a bit of survival lessons from my cousin, he declared

"Do you hear that!"

So we stopped to listen

A faint sound of water falling could be heard but it would be

Another twenty or thirty minutes before we reached the falls.

As we drew closer, the sound became a thunderous movement

And a great sense of relief came over me

Straight out of the forest into a clearing

Before our eyes

A giant, magnificent waterfall awaited us

If it wasn't for a butterfly and the voice of my doctor

Urging me to go on, I might have missed out on witnessing one of nature's

Artful sculptures…

Sitting on the rocks to rest a bit

My attention was drawn to the bottom of the falls

Before our eyes sprawled a huge pool

Colours of forest green and several shades of rock reflected on

The surface and depth of the Crystal Clear Waters.

The need to get closer became overwhelming…

Another ten to twelve feet of climbing down some jagged rocks until

I reached the waters edge

As my hands touched the cool clear water… I couldn't resist.

Discarding running shoes and socks…I plunged into the pool and started swimming

Around

I was tired no more

After a while laying on the rocks in the shallow waters

I began to experience a heightened sense of awareness

The green of the forest became greener

I couldn't tell where the entrance to this magnificence was

But there was no worry.

Looking up at the rich cerulean blue sky

The feeling of

"There is something bigger than me at work here"

I felt included in whatever was unfolding and that today

Was a day to truly live every moment…

And so I took it all in

Peace Silence Beauty

All wrapped into one

Catapulting me into the realization

"I was in the womb of Mother Nature herself

Waiting to be reborn"

Physical pain and emotional suffering

Became just a story of my life

Of lessons learned and to grow from

Rediscovering Love and Purpose as my own truth...

This was what my soul has been crying out for- all these years

After a light lunch of sandwiches and fruit

Everyone sat quietly basking in the sun, while warming up from the cool waters

Of the falls

At one point the sun became hidden by a passing cloud.

From behind us

The Big, Blue, Beautiful Butterfly

Came out of the forest again

I couldn't take my eyes off of him as he fluttered the perimeter of the clearing

As he was nearing the falls, I became concerned for his safety.

He began a dance of going in and out of the spraying mist from the cascading falls

The sun came out at that moment creating a magical rainbow and the butterfly

Continued his fluttering dance in and out of the misty waters.

This was amazing to watch!

The butterfly re-entered the forest after completing his circle and disappeared

I heard my cousin's voice saying

"It is time to go"

As we were walking back to civilization

A feeling of great strength and lack of fear permeated my being…

My Body was given a second chance of life, by improving

The flow of blood to the arteries and veins

My Mind experienced a re-birth in the womb of Mother Nature

While the spirit soared on the wings of a butterfly

I was given the gift of uniting the soul with my human self that day…

I shall forever be grateful to the Universe for creating

Such an astonishing experience

Of fulfilling a wish

I never knew I wished for…

In honour of my father

CHILDREN

"CHILDREN," I call. THIS WONDER

You must see.

Leave all your tasks

And join me in our garden

Let me point this beautiful story

Out to you

"See that flower there, see it

Opening?

See the colours hidden within

Revealing itself, unsuspecting that we watch?

"See the beauty and the grace as

Petal after petal open

All arranged

Even I don't know by whom

No jar of colours here

Each petal catching sunlight

Just enough that it may bloom

No wasting here

No hording here

"Ah smell that fragrance now

So fresh, the air is filled

See now, how fragile butterflies

Swoop close to have some tea

Now birds come visiting, heaping

Praise on the flower's beauty

And busy bees come taking up

Collections for some cause

That's not their own?

And the flower itself?

For all its life 'twil share its nectar

Give its beauty and

Its fragrance 'round.

"Here you see the lesson, CHILDREN?

See how we should grow?"

Written by R.I Bann
Shortly before his death
(1928-1973)

ABOUT THE AUTHOR

Originally from Trinidad. Residence Quebec, Canada. My joy comes from
Living in Love, beauty and purpose. I believe the painful and the mundane
present space for growth or stagnation. In this world of constant change,
I find my truth thru the eyes of Love, beauty and purpose...

Printed in the United States
By Bookmasters